ASSIGNMENT NOTEBOOK

Name:

School:

Grade:

My Passwords

Website:
Username:
Password:
Notes: Subject:

Website:
Username:
Password:
Notes: Subject:

Website:
Username:
Password:
Notes: Subject:

Website:
Username:
Password:
Notes: Subject:

Website:
Username:
Password:
Notes: Subject:

My Passwords

Website:
Username:
Password:
Notes: Subject:

Website:
Username:
Password:
Notes: Subject:

Website:
Username:
Password:
Notes: Subject:

Website:
Username:
Password:
Notes: Subject:

Website:
Username:
Password:
Notes: Subject:

Class Schedule

1st Semester

Time	Class	Teacher

Class Schedule

2nd Semester

Time	Class	Teacher

Homework planner

	Subject	Due	Homework details	Today's Date
Monday				

	Subject	Due	Homework details	Today's Date
Tuesday				

	Subject	Due	Homework details	Today's Date
Wednesday				

Homework planner

Thursday

Subject	Due	Homework details	Today's Date

Friday

Subject	Due	Homework details	Today's Date

Spelling Words

Book of the week

Homework planner

Monday

Subject	Due	Homework details	Today's Date

Tuesday

Subject	Due	Homework details	Today's Date

Wednesday

Subject	Due	Homework details	Today's Date

Homework planner

Thursday

Subject	Due	Homework details	Today's Date

Friday

Subject	Due	Homework details	Today's Date

Spelling Words

Book of the week

Homework planner

Tests this week:

	Subject	Due	Homework details	Today's Date
Monday				

	Subject	Due	Homework details	Today's Date
Tuesday				

	Subject	Due	Homework details	Today's Date
Wednesday				

Homework planner

Thursday

Subject	Due	Homework details	Today's Date

Friday

Subject	Due	Homework details	Today's Date

Spelling words

Book of the week

Homework planner

	Subject	Due	Homework details	Today's Date
Monday				

	Subject	Due	Homework details	Today's Date
Tuesday				

	Subject	Due	Homework details	Today's Date
Wednesday				

Homework planner

Thursday

Subject	Due	Homework details	Today's Date

Friday

Subject	Due	Homework details	Today's Date

Spelling words · Book of the week

Homework planner

Tests this week:

Monday

Subject	Due	Homework details	Today's Date

Tuesday

Subject	Due	Homework details	Today's Date

Wednesday

Subject	Due	Homework details	Today's Date

Homework planner

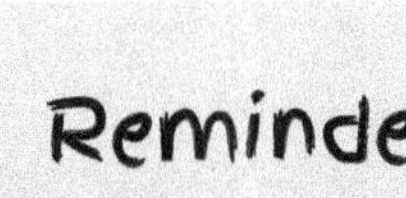

Reminder:

	Subject	Due	Homework details	Today's Date
Thursday				

	Subject	Due	Homework details	Today's Date
Friday				

Spelling words

Book of the week

Homework planner

Monday

Subject	Due	Homework details	Today's Date

Tuesday

Subject	Due	Homework details	Today's Date

Wednesday

Subject	Due	Homework details	Today's Date

Homework planner

Thursday

Subject	Due	Homework details	Today's Date

Friday

Subject	Due	Homework details	Today's Date

Spelling Words

Book of the week

Homework planner

Tests this week:

<table>
<tr><td rowspan="7">Monday</td><td>Subject</td><td>Due</td><td>Homework details</td><td>Today's Date</td></tr>
<tr><td></td><td></td><td></td><td></td></tr>
<tr><td></td><td></td><td></td><td></td></tr>
<tr><td></td><td></td><td></td><td></td></tr>
<tr><td></td><td></td><td></td><td></td></tr>
<tr><td></td><td></td><td></td><td></td></tr>
<tr><td></td><td></td><td></td><td></td></tr>
<tr><td rowspan="7">Tuesday</td><td>Subject</td><td>Due</td><td>Homework details</td><td>Today's Date</td></tr>
<tr><td></td><td></td><td></td><td></td></tr>
<tr><td></td><td></td><td></td><td></td></tr>
<tr><td></td><td></td><td></td><td></td></tr>
<tr><td></td><td></td><td></td><td></td></tr>
<tr><td></td><td></td><td></td><td></td></tr>
<tr><td></td><td></td><td></td><td></td></tr>
<tr><td rowspan="7">Wednesday</td><td>Subject</td><td>Due</td><td>Homework details</td><td>Today's Date</td></tr>
<tr><td></td><td></td><td></td><td></td></tr>
<tr><td></td><td></td><td></td><td></td></tr>
<tr><td></td><td></td><td></td><td></td></tr>
<tr><td></td><td></td><td></td><td></td></tr>
<tr><td></td><td></td><td></td><td></td></tr>
<tr><td></td><td></td><td></td><td></td></tr>
</table>

Homework planner

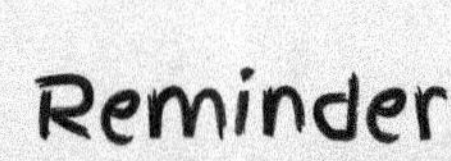

Reminder:

	Subject	Due	Homework details	Today's Date
Thursday				

	Subject	Due	Homework details	Today's Date
Friday				

Spelling Words   Book of the week

Homework planner

Tests this week:

Monday

Subject	Due	Homework details	Today's Date

Tuesday

Subject	Due	Homework details	Today's Date

Wednesday

Subject	Due	Homework details	Today's Date

Homework planner

<table>
<tr><td rowspan="6">Thursday</td><td>Subject</td><td>Due</td><td>Homework details</td><td>Today's Date</td></tr>
<tr><td></td><td></td><td></td><td></td></tr>
<tr><td></td><td></td><td></td><td></td></tr>
<tr><td></td><td></td><td></td><td></td></tr>
<tr><td></td><td></td><td></td><td></td></tr>
<tr><td></td><td></td><td></td><td></td></tr>
</table>

<table>
<tr><td rowspan="6">Friday</td><td>Subject</td><td>Due</td><td>Homework details</td><td>Today's Date</td></tr>
<tr><td></td><td></td><td></td><td></td></tr>
<tr><td></td><td></td><td></td><td></td></tr>
<tr><td></td><td></td><td></td><td></td></tr>
<tr><td></td><td></td><td></td><td></td></tr>
<tr><td></td><td></td><td></td><td></td></tr>
</table>

Spelling Words
Book of the week

Homework planner

Tests this week:

Monday

Subject	Due	Homework details	Today's Date

Tuesday

Subject	Due	Homework details	Today's Date

Wednesday

Subject	Due	Homework details	Today's Date

Homework planner

Thursday

Subject	Due	Homework details	Today's Date

Friday

Subject	Due	Homework details	Today's Date

Spelling Words   Book of the week

Homework planner

	Subject	Due	Homework details	Today's Date
Monday				

	Subject	Due	Homework details	Today's Date
Tuesday				

	Subject	Due	Homework details	Today's Date
Wednesday				

Homework planner

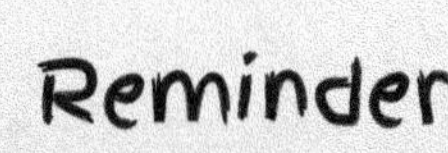

Thursday

Subject	Due	Homework details	Today's Date

Friday

Subject	Due	Homework details	Today's Date

Spelling words

Book of the week

Homework planner

Monday

Subject	Due	Homework details	Today's Date

Tuesday

Subject	Due	Homework details	Today's Date

Wednesday

Subject	Due	Homework details	Today's Date

Homework planner

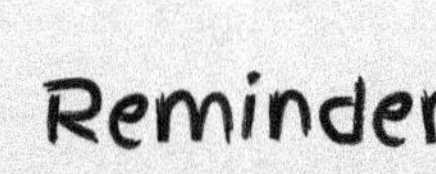

Reminder:

Thursday

Subject	Due	Homework details	Today's Date

Friday

Subject	Due	Homework details	Today's Date

Spelling words

Book of the week

Homework planner

Monday

Subject	Due	Homework details	Today's Date

Tuesday

Subject	Due	Homework details	Today's Date

Wednesday

Subject	Due	Homework details	Today's Date

Homework planner

Thursday

Subject	Due	Homework details	Today's Date

Friday

Subject	Due	Homework details	Today's Date

Spelling words

Book of the week

Homework planner

Monday

Subject	Due	Homework details	Today's Date

Tuesday

Subject	Due	Homework details	Today's Date

Wednesday

Subject	Due	Homework details	Today's Date

Homework planner

Thursday

Subject	Due	Homework details	Today's Date

Friday

Subject	Due	Homework details	Today's Date

Spelling Words

Book of the week

Homework planner

Tests this week:

Monday	Subject	Due	Homework details	Today's Date

Tuesday	Subject	Due	Homework details	Today's Date

Wednesday	Subject	Due	Homework details	Today's Date

Homework planner

Thursday

Subject	Due	Homework details	Today's Date

Friday

Subject	Due	Homework details	Today's Date

Spelling Words

Book of the week

Homework planner

Tests this week:

<table>
<tr><td rowspan="7">Monday</td><td>Subject</td><td>Due</td><td>Homework details</td><td>Today's Date</td></tr>
<tr><td></td><td></td><td></td><td></td></tr>
<tr><td></td><td></td><td></td><td></td></tr>
<tr><td></td><td></td><td></td><td></td></tr>
<tr><td></td><td></td><td></td><td></td></tr>
<tr><td></td><td></td><td></td><td></td></tr>
<tr><td></td><td></td><td></td><td></td></tr>
<tr><td rowspan="7">Tuesday</td><td>Subject</td><td>Due</td><td>Homework details</td><td>Today's Date</td></tr>
<tr><td></td><td></td><td></td><td></td></tr>
<tr><td></td><td></td><td></td><td></td></tr>
<tr><td></td><td></td><td></td><td></td></tr>
<tr><td></td><td></td><td></td><td></td></tr>
<tr><td></td><td></td><td></td><td></td></tr>
<tr><td></td><td></td><td></td><td></td></tr>
<tr><td rowspan="7">Wednesday</td><td>Subject</td><td>Due</td><td>Homework details</td><td>Today's Date</td></tr>
<tr><td></td><td></td><td></td><td></td></tr>
<tr><td></td><td></td><td></td><td></td></tr>
<tr><td></td><td></td><td></td><td></td></tr>
<tr><td></td><td></td><td></td><td></td></tr>
<tr><td></td><td></td><td></td><td></td></tr>
<tr><td></td><td></td><td></td><td></td></tr>
</table>

Homework planner

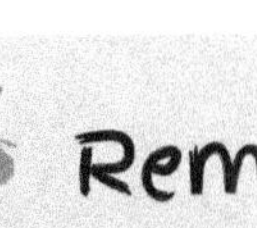

Reminder:

Thursday

Subject	Due	Homework details	Today's Date

Friday

Subject	Due	Homework details	Today's Date

Spelling words

Book of the week

Homework planner

Tests this week:

Monday

Subject	Due	Homework details	Today's Date

Tuesday

Subject	Due	Homework details	Today's Date

Wednesday

Subject	Due	Homework details	Today's Date

Homework planner

Thursday	Subject	Due	Homework details	Today's Date

Friday	Subject	Due	Homework details	Today's Date

Spelling words   Book of the week

Homework planner

Monday

Subject	Due	Homework details	Today's Date

Tuesday

Subject	Due	Homework details	Today's Date

Wednesday

Subject	Due	Homework details	Today's Date

Homework planner

Reminder:

	Subject	Due	Homework details	Today's Date
Thursday				

	Subject	Due	Homework details	Today's Date
Friday				

Spelling words

Book of the week

Homework planner

Tests this week:

<table>
<tr><td rowspan="7">Monday</td><td>Subject</td><td>Due</td><td>Homework details</td><td>Today's Date</td></tr>
<tr><td></td><td></td><td></td><td></td></tr>
<tr><td></td><td></td><td></td><td></td></tr>
<tr><td></td><td></td><td></td><td></td></tr>
<tr><td></td><td></td><td></td><td></td></tr>
<tr><td></td><td></td><td></td><td></td></tr>
<tr><td></td><td></td><td></td><td></td></tr>
<tr><td rowspan="7">Tuesday</td><td>Subject</td><td>Due</td><td>Homework details</td><td>Today's Date</td></tr>
<tr><td></td><td></td><td></td><td></td></tr>
<tr><td></td><td></td><td></td><td></td></tr>
<tr><td></td><td></td><td></td><td></td></tr>
<tr><td></td><td></td><td></td><td></td></tr>
<tr><td></td><td></td><td></td><td></td></tr>
<tr><td></td><td></td><td></td><td></td></tr>
<tr><td rowspan="7">Wednesday</td><td>Subject</td><td>Due</td><td>Homework details</td><td>Today's Date</td></tr>
<tr><td></td><td></td><td></td><td></td></tr>
<tr><td></td><td></td><td></td><td></td></tr>
<tr><td></td><td></td><td></td><td></td></tr>
<tr><td></td><td></td><td></td><td></td></tr>
<tr><td></td><td></td><td></td><td></td></tr>
<tr><td></td><td></td><td></td><td></td></tr>
</table>

Homework planner

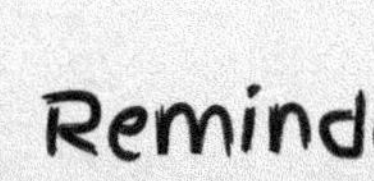

Reminder:

	Subject	Due	Homework details	Today's Date
Thursday				

	Subject	Due	Homework details	Today's Date
Friday				

Spelling words

Book of the week

Homework planner

Tests this week:

	Subject	Due	Homework details	Today's Date
Monday				

	Subject	Due	Homework details	Today's Date
Tuesday				

	Subject	Due	Homework details	Today's Date
Wednesday				

Homework planner

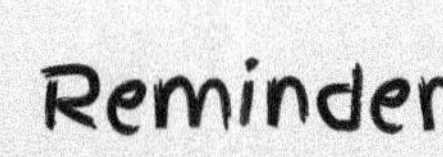

Reminder:

Thursday

Subject	Due	Homework details	Today's Date

Friday

Subject	Due	Homework details	Today's Date

Spelling words

Book of the week

Homework planner

Tests this week:

<table>
<tr><td rowspan="7" align="center">Monday</td><td>Subject</td><td>Due</td><td>Homework details</td><td>Today's Date</td></tr>
<tr><td></td><td></td><td></td><td></td></tr>
<tr><td></td><td></td><td></td><td></td></tr>
<tr><td></td><td></td><td></td><td></td></tr>
<tr><td></td><td></td><td></td><td></td></tr>
<tr><td></td><td></td><td></td><td></td></tr>
<tr><td></td><td></td><td></td><td></td></tr>
<tr><td rowspan="7" align="center">Tuesday</td><td>Subject</td><td>Due</td><td>Homework details</td><td>Today's Date</td></tr>
<tr><td></td><td></td><td></td><td></td></tr>
<tr><td></td><td></td><td></td><td></td></tr>
<tr><td></td><td></td><td></td><td></td></tr>
<tr><td></td><td></td><td></td><td></td></tr>
<tr><td></td><td></td><td></td><td></td></tr>
<tr><td></td><td></td><td></td><td></td></tr>
<tr><td rowspan="7" align="center">Wednesday</td><td>Subject</td><td>Due</td><td>Homework details</td><td>Today's Date</td></tr>
<tr><td></td><td></td><td></td><td></td></tr>
<tr><td></td><td></td><td></td><td></td></tr>
<tr><td></td><td></td><td></td><td></td></tr>
<tr><td></td><td></td><td></td><td></td></tr>
<tr><td></td><td></td><td></td><td></td></tr>
<tr><td></td><td></td><td></td><td></td></tr>
</table>

Homework planner

<table>
<tr><td rowspan="6">Thursday</td><td>Subject</td><td>Due</td><td>Homework details</td><td>Today's Date</td></tr>
<tr><td></td><td></td><td></td><td></td></tr>
<tr><td></td><td></td><td></td><td></td></tr>
<tr><td></td><td></td><td></td><td></td></tr>
<tr><td></td><td></td><td></td><td></td></tr>
<tr><td></td><td></td><td></td><td></td></tr>
</table>

<table>
<tr><td rowspan="6">Friday</td><td>Subject</td><td>Due</td><td>Homework details</td><td>Today's Date</td></tr>
<tr><td></td><td></td><td></td><td></td></tr>
<tr><td></td><td></td><td></td><td></td></tr>
<tr><td></td><td></td><td></td><td></td></tr>
<tr><td></td><td></td><td></td><td></td></tr>
<tr><td></td><td></td><td></td><td></td></tr>
</table>

Spelling Words

Book of the week

<table>
<tr><td></td><td></td><td></td><td rowspan="4"></td></tr>
<tr><td></td><td></td><td></td></tr>
<tr><td></td><td></td><td></td></tr>
<tr><td></td><td></td><td></td></tr>
</table>

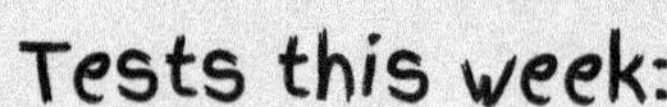

Homework planner

Monday

Subject	Due	Homework details	Today's Date

Tuesday

Subject	Due	Homework details	Today's Date

Wednesday

Subject	Due	Homework details	Today's Date

Homework planner

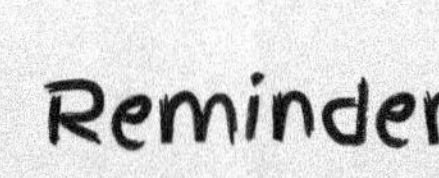

Reminder:

	Subject	Due	Homework details	Today's Date
Thursday				

	Subject	Due	Homework details	Today's Date
Friday				

Spelling words

Book of the week

Homework planner

Tests this week:

	Subject	Due	Homework details	Today's Date
Monday				

	Subject	Due	Homework details	Today's Date
Tuesday				

	Subject	Due	Homework details	Today's Date
Wednesday				

Homework planner

Reminder:

Thursday

Subject	Due	Homework details	Today's Date

Friday

Subject	Due	Homework details	Today's Date

Spelling Words

Book of the week

Homework planner

Monday

Subject	Due	Homework details	Today's Date

Tuesday

Subject	Due	Homework details	Today's Date

Wednesday

Subject	Due	Homework details	Today's Date

Homework planner

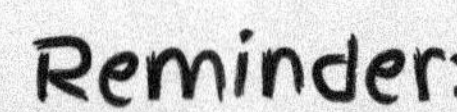

Reminder:

<table>
<tr><td rowspan="7">Thursday</td><td>Subject</td><td>Due</td><td>Homework details</td><td>Today's Date</td></tr>
<tr><td></td><td></td><td></td><td></td></tr>
<tr><td></td><td></td><td></td><td></td></tr>
<tr><td></td><td></td><td></td><td></td></tr>
<tr><td></td><td></td><td></td><td></td></tr>
<tr><td></td><td></td><td></td><td></td></tr>
<tr><td></td><td></td><td></td><td></td></tr>
</table>

<table>
<tr><td rowspan="7">Friday</td><td>Subject</td><td>Due</td><td>Homework details</td><td>Today's Date</td></tr>
<tr><td></td><td></td><td></td><td></td></tr>
<tr><td></td><td></td><td></td><td></td></tr>
<tr><td></td><td></td><td></td><td></td></tr>
<tr><td></td><td></td><td></td><td></td></tr>
<tr><td></td><td></td><td></td><td></td></tr>
<tr><td></td><td></td><td></td><td></td></tr>
</table>

Spelling words

Book of the week

Homework planner

Monday

Subject	Due	Homework details	Today's Date

Tuesday

Subject	Due	Homework details	Today's Date

Wednesday

Subject	Due	Homework details	Today's Date

Homework planner

Thursday

Subject	Due	Homework details	Today's Date

Friday

Subject	Due	Homework details	Today's Date

Spelling words

Book of the week

Homework planner

Monday

Subject	Due	Homework details	Today's Date

Tuesday

Subject	Due	Homework details	Today's Date

Wednesday

Subject	Due	Homework details	Today's Date

Homework planner

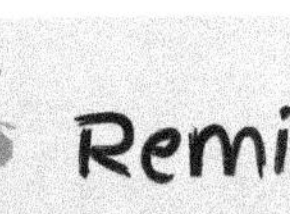

Reminder:

<table>
<tr><td rowspan="6">Thursday</td><td>Subject</td><td>Due</td><td>Homework details</td><td>Today's Date</td></tr>
<tr><td></td><td></td><td></td><td></td></tr>
<tr><td></td><td></td><td></td><td></td></tr>
<tr><td></td><td></td><td></td><td></td></tr>
<tr><td></td><td></td><td></td><td></td></tr>
<tr><td></td><td></td><td></td><td></td></tr>
<tr><td rowspan="6">Friday</td><td>Subject</td><td>Due</td><td>Homework details</td><td>Today's Date</td></tr>
<tr><td></td><td></td><td></td><td></td></tr>
<tr><td></td><td></td><td></td><td></td></tr>
<tr><td></td><td></td><td></td><td></td></tr>
<tr><td></td><td></td><td></td><td></td></tr>
<tr><td></td><td></td><td></td><td></td></tr>
</table>

Spelling Words

Book of the Week

<table>
<tr><td></td><td></td><td rowspan="4"></td></tr>
<tr><td></td><td></td></tr>
<tr><td></td><td></td></tr>
<tr><td></td><td></td></tr>
</table>

Homework planner

Monday

Subject	Due	Homework details	Today's Date

Tuesday

Subject	Due	Homework details	Today's Date

Wednesday

Subject	Due	Homework details	Today's Date

Homework planner

Thursday	Subject	Due	Homework details	Today's Date

Friday	Subject	Due	Homework details	Today's Date

Spelling words

Book of the week

Homework planner

Tests this week:

<table>
<tr><td rowspan="6">Monday</td><td>Subject</td><td>Due</td><td>Homework details</td><td>Today's Date</td></tr>
<tr><td></td><td></td><td></td><td></td></tr>
<tr><td></td><td></td><td></td><td></td></tr>
<tr><td></td><td></td><td></td><td></td></tr>
<tr><td></td><td></td><td></td><td></td></tr>
<tr><td></td><td></td><td></td><td></td></tr>
<tr><td rowspan="6">Tuesday</td><td>Subject</td><td>Due</td><td>Homework details</td><td>Today's Date</td></tr>
<tr><td></td><td></td><td></td><td></td></tr>
<tr><td></td><td></td><td></td><td></td></tr>
<tr><td></td><td></td><td></td><td></td></tr>
<tr><td></td><td></td><td></td><td></td></tr>
<tr><td></td><td></td><td></td><td></td></tr>
<tr><td rowspan="6">Wednesday</td><td>Subject</td><td>Due</td><td>Homework details</td><td>Today's Date</td></tr>
<tr><td></td><td></td><td></td><td></td></tr>
<tr><td></td><td></td><td></td><td></td></tr>
<tr><td></td><td></td><td></td><td></td></tr>
<tr><td></td><td></td><td></td><td></td></tr>
<tr><td></td><td></td><td></td><td></td></tr>
</table>

Homework planner

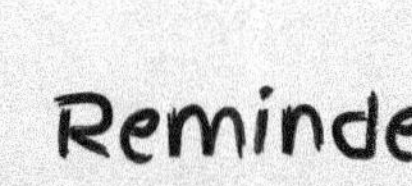

Reminder:

Thursday	Subject	Due	Homework details	Today's Date

Friday	Subject	Due	Homework details	Today's Date

Spelling Words

Book of the week

Homework planner

Monday

Subject	Due	Homework details	Today's Date

Tuesday

Subject	Due	Homework details	Today's Date

Wednesday

Subject	Due	Homework details	Today's Date

Homework planner

Reminder:

<table>
<tr><td rowspan="6">Thursday</td><td>Subject</td><td>Due</td><td>Homework details</td><td>Today's Date</td></tr>
<tr><td></td><td></td><td></td><td></td></tr>
<tr><td></td><td></td><td></td><td></td></tr>
<tr><td></td><td></td><td></td><td></td></tr>
<tr><td></td><td></td><td></td><td></td></tr>
<tr><td></td><td></td><td></td><td></td></tr>
</table>

<table>
<tr><td rowspan="6">Friday</td><td>Subject</td><td>Due</td><td>Homework details</td><td>Today's Date</td></tr>
<tr><td></td><td></td><td></td><td></td></tr>
<tr><td></td><td></td><td></td><td></td></tr>
<tr><td></td><td></td><td></td><td></td></tr>
<tr><td></td><td></td><td></td><td></td></tr>
<tr><td></td><td></td><td></td><td></td></tr>
</table>

Spelling words

Book of the week

Homework planner

Monday

Subject	Due	Homework details	Today's Date

Tuesday

Subject	Due	Homework details	Today's Date

Wednesday

Subject	Due	Homework details	Today's Date

Homework planner

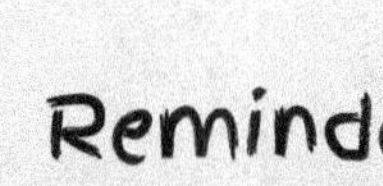

Reminder:

Thursday

Subject	Due	Homework details	Today's Date

Friday

Subject	Due	Homework details	Today's Date

Spelling Words

Book of the Week

Homework planner

Tests this week:

	Subject	Due	Homework details	Today's Date
Monday				

	Subject	Due	Homework details	Today's Date
Tuesday				

	Subject	Due	Homework details	Today's Date
Wednesday				

Homework planner

Reminder:

	Subject	Due	Homework details	Today's Date
Thursday				

	Subject	Due	Homework details	Today's Date
Friday				

Spelling words

Book of the week

Homework planner

Monday

Subject	Due	Homework details	Today's Date

Tuesday

Subject	Due	Homework details	Today's Date

Wednesday

Subject	Due	Homework details	Today's Date

Homework planner

Reminder:

	Subject	Due	Homework details	Today's Date
Thursday				

	Subject	Due	Homework details	Today's Date
Friday				

Spelling Words

Book of the week

Homework planner

Tests this week:

Monday

Subject	Due	Homework details	Today's Date

Tuesday

Subject	Due	Homework details	Today's Date

Wednesday

Subject	Due	Homework details	Today's Date

Homework planner

Reminder:

	Subject	Due	Homework details	Today's Date
Thursday				

	Subject	Due	Homework details	Today's Date
Friday				

Spelling words

Book of the week

Homework planner

Tests this week:

<table>
<tr><td rowspan="7">Monday</td><td>Subject</td><td>Due</td><td>Homework details</td><td>Today's Date</td></tr>
<tr><td></td><td></td><td></td><td></td></tr>
<tr><td></td><td></td><td></td><td></td></tr>
<tr><td></td><td></td><td></td><td></td></tr>
<tr><td></td><td></td><td></td><td></td></tr>
<tr><td></td><td></td><td></td><td></td></tr>
<tr><td></td><td></td><td></td><td></td></tr>
<tr><td rowspan="7">Tuesday</td><td>Subject</td><td>Due</td><td>Homework details</td><td>Today's Date</td></tr>
<tr><td></td><td></td><td></td><td></td></tr>
<tr><td></td><td></td><td></td><td></td></tr>
<tr><td></td><td></td><td></td><td></td></tr>
<tr><td></td><td></td><td></td><td></td></tr>
<tr><td></td><td></td><td></td><td></td></tr>
<tr><td></td><td></td><td></td><td></td></tr>
<tr><td rowspan="7">Wednesday</td><td>Subject</td><td>Due</td><td>Homework details</td><td>Today's Date</td></tr>
<tr><td></td><td></td><td></td><td></td></tr>
<tr><td></td><td></td><td></td><td></td></tr>
<tr><td></td><td></td><td></td><td></td></tr>
<tr><td></td><td></td><td></td><td></td></tr>
<tr><td></td><td></td><td></td><td></td></tr>
<tr><td></td><td></td><td></td><td></td></tr>
</table>

Homework planner

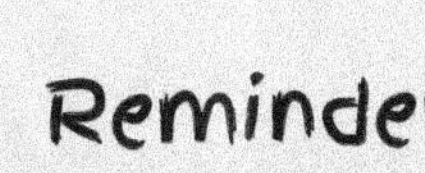

	Subject	Due	Homework details	Today's Date
Thursday				

	Subject	Due	Homework details	Today's Date
Friday				

Spelling words

Book of the week

Homework planner

Tests this week:

<table>
<tr><td rowspan="7">Monday</td><td>Subject</td><td>Due</td><td>Homework details</td><td>Today's Date</td></tr>
<tr><td></td><td></td><td></td><td></td></tr>
<tr><td></td><td></td><td></td><td></td></tr>
<tr><td></td><td></td><td></td><td></td></tr>
<tr><td></td><td></td><td></td><td></td></tr>
<tr><td></td><td></td><td></td><td></td></tr>
<tr><td></td><td></td><td></td><td></td></tr>
<tr><td rowspan="7">Tuesday</td><td>Subject</td><td>Due</td><td>Homework details</td><td>Today's Date</td></tr>
<tr><td></td><td></td><td></td><td></td></tr>
<tr><td></td><td></td><td></td><td></td></tr>
<tr><td></td><td></td><td></td><td></td></tr>
<tr><td></td><td></td><td></td><td></td></tr>
<tr><td></td><td></td><td></td><td></td></tr>
<tr><td></td><td></td><td></td><td></td></tr>
<tr><td rowspan="7">Wednesday</td><td>Subject</td><td>Due</td><td>Homework details</td><td>Today's Date</td></tr>
<tr><td></td><td></td><td></td><td></td></tr>
<tr><td></td><td></td><td></td><td></td></tr>
<tr><td></td><td></td><td></td><td></td></tr>
<tr><td></td><td></td><td></td><td></td></tr>
<tr><td></td><td></td><td></td><td></td></tr>
<tr><td></td><td></td><td></td><td></td></tr>
</table>

Homework planner

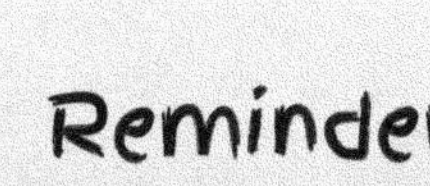

Reminder:

<table>
<tr><td rowspan="6">Thursday</td><td>Subject</td><td>Due</td><td>Homework details</td><td>Today's Date</td></tr>
<tr><td></td><td></td><td></td><td></td></tr>
<tr><td></td><td></td><td></td><td></td></tr>
<tr><td></td><td></td><td></td><td></td></tr>
<tr><td></td><td></td><td></td><td></td></tr>
<tr><td></td><td></td><td></td><td></td></tr>
</table>

<table>
<tr><td rowspan="6">Friday</td><td>Subject</td><td>Due</td><td>Homework details</td><td>Today's Date</td></tr>
<tr><td></td><td></td><td></td><td></td></tr>
<tr><td></td><td></td><td></td><td></td></tr>
<tr><td></td><td></td><td></td><td></td></tr>
<tr><td></td><td></td><td></td><td></td></tr>
<tr><td></td><td></td><td></td><td></td></tr>
</table>

Spelling Words   Book of the week

Homework planner

Tests this week:

Monday

Subject	Due	Homework details	Today's Date

Tuesday

Subject	Due	Homework details	Today's Date

Wednesday

Subject	Due	Homework details	Today's Date

Homework planner

Reminder:

<table>
<tr><td rowspan="7">Thursday</td><td>Subject</td><td>Due</td><td>Homework details</td><td>Today's Date</td></tr>
<tr><td></td><td></td><td></td><td></td></tr>
<tr><td></td><td></td><td></td><td></td></tr>
<tr><td></td><td></td><td></td><td></td></tr>
<tr><td></td><td></td><td></td><td></td></tr>
<tr><td></td><td></td><td></td><td></td></tr>
<tr><td></td><td></td><td></td><td></td></tr>
</table>

<table>
<tr><td rowspan="7">Friday</td><td>Subject</td><td>Due</td><td>Homework details</td><td>Today's Date</td></tr>
<tr><td></td><td></td><td></td><td></td></tr>
<tr><td></td><td></td><td></td><td></td></tr>
<tr><td></td><td></td><td></td><td></td></tr>
<tr><td></td><td></td><td></td><td></td></tr>
<tr><td></td><td></td><td></td><td></td></tr>
<tr><td></td><td></td><td></td><td></td></tr>
</table>

Spelling Words — Book of the Week

Homework planner

Monday

Subject	Due	Homework details	Today's Date

Tuesday

Subject	Due	Homework details	Today's Date

Wednesday

Subject	Due	Homework details	Today's Date

Homework planner

Reminder:

<table>
<tr><th></th><th>Subject</th><th>Due</th><th>Homework details</th><th>Today's Date</th></tr>
<tr><td rowspan="6">Thursday</td><td></td><td></td><td></td><td></td></tr>
<tr><td></td><td></td><td></td><td></td></tr>
<tr><td></td><td></td><td></td><td></td></tr>
<tr><td></td><td></td><td></td><td></td></tr>
<tr><td></td><td></td><td></td><td></td></tr>
<tr><td></td><td></td><td></td><td></td></tr>
</table>

<table>
<tr><th></th><th>Subject</th><th>Due</th><th>Homework details</th><th>Today's Date</th></tr>
<tr><td rowspan="6">Friday</td><td></td><td></td><td></td><td></td></tr>
<tr><td></td><td></td><td></td><td></td></tr>
<tr><td></td><td></td><td></td><td></td></tr>
<tr><td></td><td></td><td></td><td></td></tr>
<tr><td></td><td></td><td></td><td></td></tr>
<tr><td></td><td></td><td></td><td></td></tr>
</table>

Spelling words

Book of the week

<table>
<tr><td></td><td></td><td rowspan="4"></td></tr>
<tr><td></td><td></td></tr>
<tr><td></td><td></td></tr>
<tr><td></td><td></td></tr>
</table>

Homework planner

Monday

Subject	Due	Homework details	Today's Date

Tuesday

Subject	Due	Homework details	Today's Date

Wednesday

Subject	Due	Homework details	Today's Date

Homework planner

	Subject	Due	Homework details	Today's Date
Thursday				

	Subject	Due	Homework details	Today's Date
Friday				

Spelling Words

Book of the week

Homework planner

	Subject	Due	Homework details	Today's Date
Monday				

	Subject	Due	Homework details	Today's Date
Tuesday				

	Subject	Due	Homework details	Today's Date
Wednesday				

Homework planner

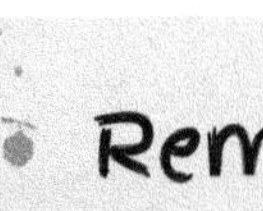

Thursday	Subject	Due	Homework details	Today's Date

Friday	Subject	Due	Homework details	Today's Date

Spelling Words   Book of the week

Homework planner

Tests this week:

	Subject	Due	Homework details	Today's Date
Monday				

	Subject	Due	Homework details	Today's Date
Tuesday				

	Subject	Due	Homework details	Today's Date
Wednesday				

Homework planner

Reminder:

<table>
<tr><td rowspan="6">Thursday</td><td>Subject</td><td>Due</td><td>Homework details</td><td>Today's Date</td></tr>
<tr><td></td><td></td><td></td><td></td></tr>
<tr><td></td><td></td><td></td><td></td></tr>
<tr><td></td><td></td><td></td><td></td></tr>
<tr><td></td><td></td><td></td><td></td></tr>
<tr><td></td><td></td><td></td><td></td></tr>
</table>

<table>
<tr><td rowspan="6">Friday</td><td>Subject</td><td>Due</td><td>Homework details</td><td>Today's Date</td></tr>
<tr><td></td><td></td><td></td><td></td></tr>
<tr><td></td><td></td><td></td><td></td></tr>
<tr><td></td><td></td><td></td><td></td></tr>
<tr><td></td><td></td><td></td><td></td></tr>
<tr><td></td><td></td><td></td><td></td></tr>
</table>

Spelling Words

Book of the week

Homework planner

Monday

Subject	Due	Homework details	Today's Date

Tuesday

Subject	Due	Homework details	Today's Date

Wednesday

Subject	Due	Homework details	Today's Date

Homework planner

Reminder:

Subject	Due	Homework details	Today's Date

Thursday

Subject	Due	Homework details	Today's Date

Friday

Spelling Words

Book of the week

Homework planner

Tests this week:

<table>
<tr><td rowspan="7">Monday</td><td>Subject</td><td>Due</td><td>Homework details</td><td>Today's Date</td></tr>
<tr><td></td><td></td><td></td><td></td></tr>
<tr><td></td><td></td><td></td><td></td></tr>
<tr><td></td><td></td><td></td><td></td></tr>
<tr><td></td><td></td><td></td><td></td></tr>
<tr><td></td><td></td><td></td><td></td></tr>
<tr><td></td><td></td><td></td><td></td></tr>
<tr><td rowspan="7">Tuesday</td><td>Subject</td><td>Due</td><td>Homework details</td><td>Today's Date</td></tr>
<tr><td></td><td></td><td></td><td></td></tr>
<tr><td></td><td></td><td></td><td></td></tr>
<tr><td></td><td></td><td></td><td></td></tr>
<tr><td></td><td></td><td></td><td></td></tr>
<tr><td></td><td></td><td></td><td></td></tr>
<tr><td></td><td></td><td></td><td></td></tr>
<tr><td rowspan="7">Wednesday</td><td>Subject</td><td>Due</td><td>Homework details</td><td>Today's Date</td></tr>
<tr><td></td><td></td><td></td><td></td></tr>
<tr><td></td><td></td><td></td><td></td></tr>
<tr><td></td><td></td><td></td><td></td></tr>
<tr><td></td><td></td><td></td><td></td></tr>
<tr><td></td><td></td><td></td><td></td></tr>
<tr><td></td><td></td><td></td><td></td></tr>
</table>

Homework planner

Reminder:

	Subject	Due	Homework details	Today's Date
Thursday				

	Subject	Due	Homework details	Today's Date
Friday				

Spelling Words   Book of the Week

Homework planner

Tests this week:

	Subject	Due	Homework details	Today's Date
Monday				

	Subject	Due	Homework details	Today's Date
Tuesday				

	Subject	Due	Homework details	Today's Date
Wednesday				

Homework planner

Thursday

Subject	Due	Homework details	Today's Date

Friday

Subject	Due	Homework details	Today's Date

Spelling Words

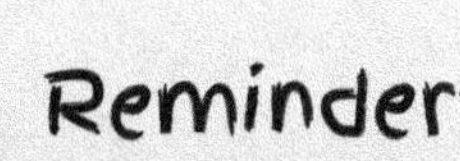

Book of the week

Homework planner

Monday

Subject	Due	Homework details	Today's Date

Tuesday

Subject	Due	Homework details	Today's Date

Wednesday

Subject	Due	Homework details	Today's Date

Homework planner

Reminder:

Thursday

Subject	Due	Homework details	Today's Date

Friday

Subject	Due	Homework details	Today's Date

Spelling Words

Book of the week

Homework planner

	Subject	Due	Homework details	Today's Date
Monday				

	Subject	Due	Homework details	Today's Date
Tuesday				

	Subject	Due	Homework details	Today's Date
Wednesday				

Homewrk planner

Thursday

Subject	Due	Homework details	Today's Date

Friday

Subject	Due	Homework details	Today's Date

Spelling words

Book of the week

Homework planner

Monday

Subject	Due	Homework details	Today's Date

Tuesday

Subject	Due	Homework details	Today's Date

Wednesday

Subject	Due	Homework details	Today's Date

Homework planner

Reminder:

	Subject	Due	Homework details	Today's Date
Thursday				

	Subject	Due	Homework details	Today's Date
Friday				

Spelling Words

Book of the Week

School Calendar September to January

	September	October	November	December	January
16					
17					
18					
19					
20					
21					
22					
23					
24					
25					
26					
27					
28					
29					
30					
31					

Record Special Projects, Book Report Deadlines and/or Special Events!

School Calendar September to January

	September	October	November	December	January
16					
17					
18					
19					
20					
21					
22					
23					
24					
25					
26					
27					
28					
29					
30					
31					

Record Special Projects, Book Report Deadlines and/or Special Events!

School Calendar February to June

	February	March	April	May	June
1					
2					
3					
4					
5					
6					
7					
8					
9					
10					
11					
12					
13					
14					
15					

Record Special Projects, Book Report Deadlines and/or Special Events!

School Calendar February to June

	February	March	April	May	June
16					
17					
18					
19					
20					
21					
22					
23					
24					
25					
26					
27					
28					
29					
30					
31					

Record Special Projects, Book Report Deadlines and/or Special Events!

My Notes

My Notes

My Notes

My Notes

My Notes

My Notes

My Notes

Record Your Grades

1st and 2nd Quarters

Subject	Quarter		Quarter
	1		1
	2		2
	1		1
	2		2
	1		1
	2		2
	1		1
	2		2
	1		1
	2		2
	1		1
	2		2
	1		1
	2		2
	1		1
	2		2

Record Your Grades

3rd and 4th Quarters

Subject	Quarter												Quarter
	3												3
	4												4
	3												3
	4												4
	3												3
	4												4
	3												3
	4												4
	3												3
	4												4
	3												3
	4												4
	3												3
	4												4
	3												3
	4												4

CREATEPUBLICATION

Thank you!

As a small family company, your feedback is very important to us.

Please let us know how you like our book at: